The
Bridge
Builders

The Bridge Builders

*Photographs and Documents
of the Raising of the
San Francisco Bay Bridge
1934–1936*

Pomegranate

Peter Stackpole

with an afterword by Anita Ventura Mozley

Published by Pomegranate Artbooks,
Box 980, Corte Madera, Calif. 94925

Photographs and text © 1984 Peter Stackpole
The Man and the Bridge © 1984 Anita Ventura Mozley

fronticepiece photo: At the top of a tower bridgemen prepare to push a
preassembled section of the catwalk into place

Designed by Bonnie Jean Smetts

ISBN 0-87654-000-0
0-87654-001-9 (hardcover)
LC 84-061886

Printed in Singapore

Dedication

I DEDICATE THIS BOOK to Joe Walton and the raising gang because they watched over me and gave me the courage to climb with them to see their world. Were it not for a kind of hero worship for all the bridgemen, as seen through the eyes of a twenty-one year old, I might not have attempted these photographs.

Joe Walton's story tells a lot about the itinerant American high-steel men of the thirties: the kind of men they were, going from job to job during hard times, accepting low pay and real danger. They were the elite group of specialists who accepted the risks associated with their tremendous projects. I still have feelings of hero worship toward these men, because I was privileged to get close to them, to watch them perform, with their nerves of steel, and I want to show in this book the faces of these long-forgotten men.

Today we race across the spans of bridges in our vehicles, unmindful of the sacrifices made to make this possible. To those men who lost their lives on the job I must also dedicate this book. I knew a few of them and can still see their faces against the steel, the concrete, and the water, working with the raising gang until their fateful moment. Twenty-three of them died on the San Francisco-Oakland Bay Bridge and fourteen on the Golden Gate Bridge.

Few of my heroes were more than distant specks against the sky in the eyes of the public who watched the growth of the giant spans with wonder and some skepticism. It took pride of accomplishment, flawless teamwork, and a daring that was uniquely American to belong to The Bridgebuilders.

—Peter Stackpole
Oakland, California, June 1983

Contents

When They Built the Bay Bridge

by Peter Stackpole

"It can't be done."

"It will never work."

The old ones on the ferry boat, commuting to work every day, watched the towers rise in disbelief. The same words came from the derelicts on the waterfront. They stood in little groups, in their soiled and torn overcoats, and watched the Bay Bridge grow.

It was the fall of 1934, and the effects of the Great Depression were visible everywhere in the groups of middle-aged men with nothing to do.

At the age of twenty-one, I was two years out of high school, without work, and facing uncertain times. On this particular day, I was riding the Oakland-San Francisco ferry boat—a good place to think things over. I wore a dark blue corduroy jacket with big pockets into which I had placed film and my prized possession: a Model C Leica camera. The small camera was new then, and I had been using it candid-style on people. Mostly experimental.

From the port side of the ferry I watched the beginning of the bridge tower and the swirling smoke from the rivet oven. Suddenly the notion came to me. It came so clearly it seemed already a fact that my camera work would take a new direction. It was just a matter of doing it.

Soon the ferry docked at Pier 24 where a sign read "American Bridge Company." Red and black painted tugs were taking workers out to the five bridge piers in the Bay. I sat for a long time on an iron cleat watching the bridgemen with a sort of boyish admiration, and the camera around my neck made me noticeable before long. One of the bridgemen asked, "Why don't you shoot some pictures of the job, kid?"

"But how?" I inquired.

"Hell, kid. Just hop on the launch the next time the gang goes out. Nobody will bother you."

His name was Joe Walton and his advice was good, because soon I was on my way out to tower W-3, where the steel was already up to road level.

Waterfront men discuss the growing span as seen from a fire boat and pier 24.

Jim Ward, superintendent, American Bridge Company.

The roar from the riveting was deafening, and everyone was so busy I went unnoticed when I took the first few pictures. Those first exposures told me that the impulse I had felt—telling me to go out to the bridge site—was correct, and I became wildly excited.

At quitting time we returned to Pier 24 and my friend Joe Walton introduced me to three more bridgemen: Jeff and Hank, and Whitey Reeves. They all wanted me to come back and take their pictures at work.

One day I followed Joe up some shaky steel ladders inside the box truss which zigzags between the tower legs.

"Just keep one hand and one foot on the ladder at all times and don't look at anything except what you are doing," advised Joe.

I followed him to the top, panting and sweating. Joe grabbed a wooden box with signal switches and put on some earphones and a mouthpiece. He began talking to the hoist operator far below, giving him the white light to start raising another forty-ton tower section.

"Big load coming up," said Joe. Jeff and Hank and the others waited with their tapered pins and buckets of bolts and nuts while the hammerhead crane slowly raised and placed the heavy section in place. All the holes lined up perfectly, and soon the air became noisy again with bolt-tightening guns securing the huge member in place. Later, the bolts were removed one by one to be replaced by rivets. With that section in place, it was lunchtime. Jeff emerged from an opening in the heavy member with his lunchbox, which he'd tied inside the load when it was down on the tower base.

The sweat on my skin had turned to chill, but I had become so engrossed in photographing that it hadn't occurred to me to be frightened by the height. There was something reassuring about being accepted by Joe and the others.

"Hey, take my picture," came a voice from above. We were sitting on the cross member at the top of the tower—some 530 feet above the Bay—and here was this guy at the very top of the stationary derrick boom above us, ready to slide down a cable out to the end of an I-bar stiffener, which extended about thirty feet out in space away from the tower top.

In time I learned that it wasn't uncommon for a bridgeman to grow impatient with waiting for the elevator and to slide down a bare cable to catch an earlier boat to shore. This practice stopped when one day a guy was sliding down a cable from the top and his gloves hit an oily section. He couldn't break his speed. The cable burned through his gloves and he hit the tower base.

There were also many casualties from falling objects. Walking around the base of the towers was particularly dangerous, as I was advised one day when I

Joe Walton, signalman, astride a cable saddle

Waterfront skeptics

encountered a formidable Irishman named Jim Ward. He was the boss of the raising gang.

"Hey you!" he hollered. "What are you doing out here without a hard hat, and what are you doing here anyway?" This was about the third time I'd sneaked out, and I feared right then that the end had come. I showed him a couple of pictures I'd taken and threw some names at him like Tim Pflueger, architect of the bridge approaches, who had liked some of my pictures.

Somehow he warmed a bit, but he warned: "Don't come back until you have something to put on your head, even if it's a chamber pot—and you'd better get a pass, too."

Jim Ward is today a legend among high-steel men. He was tough, respected, and somewhat feared. Ward lost his life on the job a few years later when a huge cantilever section fell into the river near Hartford, Connecticut, with him on it. "He lost the job," is the way bridgemen put it.

Alone, one day, I found myself on the catwalk which was made of nothing more than heavy cyclone-fence wire suspended on four support cables. I was

heading between towers W-5 and W-6, when at the bottom of the dip there was an incomplete section about eight feet long with no fence wire to walk on—just the four cables. It was quitting time, and the choice was to walk back over three tower tops and down to the San Francisco anchorage, or somehow cross that open space on the bare cables to the continued sections of fence wire, walk over the top of tower W-6 and then down to Yerba Buena Island to an earlier departure on the tug.

  I sat there on the catwalk for five minutes wondering what to do, and suddenly I remembered what Joe told me. "Don't look at anything else, just watch what you are doing." I waited another few minutes until a ferry passed from underneath, so as not to be distracted, and began to shinny across, worrying mostly about losing things from my pockets. It was a great relief to finally sink my fingers into the wire mesh at the other side.

Payday meant many things to the bridgemen. At Pier 24 they spread out in many directions, eager for another fling at their fun city—"Frisco," as they called it. They came from Ohio, Indiana, and Iowa, and there were a few Mohawks from upstate New York. In front of Pier 2, horns would toot in the waiting cars because the prostitutes knew it was payday too, and the bridgemen would pile into their cars in threes and fives to be carted off to South of Market hotels for a little diversion.

What joys we had in those days, despite the Depression. We rode that Key System train down a spit of land, holding our noses as we passed the sewer gas rising up from the mud flats on our right, while out of the train window on the left we'd see clumps of California poppies.

We walked with our group off the train down the ramp to the squeaking gangplank and onto a vibrating ferry with its churning propeller pushing it against the narrow end of the slip. Once inside we sought out familiar faces in the dining room to join for coffee. A dish of corned beef and poached egg didn't cost more than 35 cents, and it was the best around. I sometimes sat down and chattted with Bart Crum, a local attorney, and Joseph Henry Jackson, literary editor of the *Chronicle*. It was a rewarding, much anticipated, beginning and ending to a day.

Inside the entrance to the Ferry Building in San Francisco was a juke box that featured a violin, and the place smelled of popcorn, except when the fragrance of flowers at the stand outside drifted in. Suddenly the door slid open and we walked beside a drafty freight area to board the ferryboat, *Hayward*.

Looking upward from the aft top deck, an old man looked at the bridge and the following gulls, until the *Hayward* passed under the span. Instinctively, he put his hat back on his head and went inside, walking past the reddish color contoured cherry and mahogany benches, the white-enameled walls, and the neatly folded life preservers.

Perhaps he knew that we would lose these things to inevitable change, and that his commuting days on the bay were almost over. As the ferry passed under the span's shadow, he may have chilled at the thought that a way of life he had taken for granted was about to end.

Looking Back
with Joe Walton

as told to Peter Stackpole

Joe Walton: Walton not only worked on the Bay Bridge, but on the Golden Gate and Richmond-San Rafael Bridges as well.

First, when I went to New York City, I worked on the Empire State Building. We started out in the hole there, and we had eighteen guy derricks at once in the hole, that's how big it was. I think we went up about twelve stories. Then I heard they were going out on strike, so I knew some guys who were working on the Kill van Kull Bridge. They were working on Saturdays making $87.57 a week, so I quit the Empire State Building and went over to the Kill van Kull. That's where I had my fingers taken off. This big traveler ran on the top course of the bridge. It traveled on railroad tracks, and when we was moving the traveler ahead, we reaved up two sets of two-inch hemp lines on one side and two on the other. Two lead lines came in and two big drums would run on the engine, and there were niggerheads on both sides.

Well, we took a strain after we got the falls laid out and hooked up, then we took up some slack and took a strain on each set of falls. I had my one spool full and had the line tied off and had the other spool almost full, and I had just a partial strain. I had my hands down on the lead line on top, gripping the bight underneath, and the man on the other side, he wanted to take more strain on his rig. Instead of him hollering, "Hey, Joe, I want more power," he just motioned the engineer. It was a hell of a cold day and he was having trouble with the engine. It wasn't hitting on all cylinders, and he had his throttle cranked almost wide open. When he went ahead on it my hand was almost a foot in front, see, and it took me right in. Took two fingers off my right hand—pulled them off the sockets and I cut loose the bight of the line. Well, I wouldn't turn the other line loose because, well, if I turned mine loose the whole rig was liable to go down over that arch and we'd all be killed. The whole derrick would have went down. We were up 400 and some feet.

Another time, we were building a trestle over the main line of the Pennsylvania Railroad and I got knocked off that bridge. A rivet gun was lying on the top girder and a fellow hit the air and the plunger hit me on the hard part of the heel and knocked both feet from under me and down over the side I went. Luckily, the bank was tapered down about 45 degrees, and I lit on the bank and then I rolled all the way down to the river. That was only about 80 feet up. I must have rolled some 35 feet. If I'd been over the railroad tracks, the fall would have killed me.

Then I had a job up the Allegheny River. We built sand dredges, derrick barges, and then I come into Pittsburgh, went to work at Pittsburgh Bridge Iron on the old Black Diamond Steel Mill. We done a lot of remodeling work in there. Finished that job and didn't have no job to go to. Ran into a fellow there and we run into Scranton, Pennsylvania. I wanted to go into New York, so I walked outside of Scranton, caught a freight train, went over the mountains into Carbondale, and I went to work in a damn coal mine running a donkey engine and bringing the cars out of the mountain. I'd set the brakes on about every third car, and I made a couple or three trips out of there with no trouble at all. Next time I didn't set the damn brakes and I really come out the mouth of that tunnel. They got what you call a slag dump. I came around the bend all right, but the cars just kept going down into the slag dump. I never even stopped to get my money, I just kept on going.

Joe Walton signaling to crew below.

It was at dusk just before the fall of the year, and I had enough money to get something to eat in a restaurant, and I asked if anyone was going towards Pittsburgh. A guy said, "You mean to tell me you're going to hitch-hike over the mountains?" I had no other choice. "Well I wouldn't do it. I wouldn't do it if I were you." That was a time when nobody would stop to pick up a hitch-hiker, they were having so much trouble.

God damn, I run, I walked, it started to rain sleet. Finally I come to this shack and one faint light was in it and I said, "Uh-oh," and I went up on the front porch and knocked on the door thinking maybe somebody will let me in. All at once I hear a window up on the second floor raise up and a guy sticks his head out.

"What in the hell do you want?"

I says, "I'm wringing wet, and I'm almost froze to death and I'd like to come in and get dry and rest up a bit."

He said, "The people who live here are not here, they're back in Gettysburg or someplace."

Joe Walton monitoring progress of upcoming load

I said, "What in the hell are you doing here, then?"

He said, "I'm not going to let you in."

Then I fell off the porch and into a clump of bushes and he shut the damn window. I figured he might have shot me, but by god there was a roof overhead so I lay down on the front porch cold, wet and tired, with feet, legs and ankles swelling, and I was shaking like a leaf. I got up because if I lay there I'd freeze to death, so I started out again and when it quit raining I thought, well Jesus, if I can get over this hill I'll come into a little village or something.

When I got over the hill there was nothing on the other side, and boy, I'm telling you, by the time I got home my feet was aching. I climbed up on the fence to rest myself. I couldn't sit down on the road, it was wet, you know. I'm running most of the time thinking I'm going to come to a barn or something where I can get inside. I had to hold onto the fence to get the stiffness out of my legs.

Finally I hit home and my Dad said, "Goddamn, son, where in the hell have you been?"

"You didn't send me any money so I had to get home the best I could."

I rested up a bit, then I went on to Philadelphia and drove cabs there for a while. That's where I went to work on the Delaware River Bridge.

I was one that always wanted to make the biggest job and the farthest away it was it didn't matter to me. I knew they was going to build the San Francisco-Oakland Bay Bridge and I wanted to come west. The only way I knew to get there was to drive my Buick convertible.

My brother said, "You mean to tell me you are going to drive that goddamn thing to San Francisco?"

I said, "Sure."

"With them tires and the condition they're in?"

It was a Buick '29 sports-model deluxe roadster.

I left home in Midland, Pennsylvania, and like a hayseed, you know, you think you can drive forever, and I kept driving and driving. I come to Indianapolis, St. Louis, and I get to Kansas City, Kansas, when it starts snowing, and I run into a hell of a blizzard out on them plains. I said, "Uh-oh, I'm going to run into trouble," and it's snowing so hard it's packing on the roadside, you know. This is coming out the old Lincoln highway. They wasn't any freeways then. I got on the wrong road and back in Kansas it's a mile this way and a mile that way. It's all in sections. Finally I got back on the road and the wind blew the eisenglass out of my side curtain and I pull into Pleasanton, Kansas. I found a little hotel and got a room and got up the next morning and looked outside and there's my car—it looked like a mountain of snow.

What am I going to do now? I still got a little bit of money, so I get out and started cleaning all the snow off the car and I take off. I come into Oklahoma City. I had a friend there who was a dentist. He made me acquainted with his girl friend, and we went out to dinner. Next day I took off heading west, and I get to El Paso, Texas, so I checked into the El Paso Hotel, and I thought, "Gee, I'm this close to Mexico." I didn't know that they had gambling over there. I walked across the bridge and the first thing I see was a gambling place. I didn't know nothing about gambling. I never been in a gambling joint. I played penny ante and poker and stud poker and shot craps before, so I started playing roulette. I was playing the Mexican flag and the American flag, and I drank some tequila. I heard about tequila. I went broke and there I am. I went back to the hotel and thought, "Jesus, I can't get out of here until I pay my bill and I've got to go to San Francisco." So I sent

Walton helping the raising gang to rotate the stiffleg derrick on the tower top

Walton pushing aside a tackle block inside the center well of a tower

a telegram home for fifty bucks and do you know I made it on fifty bucks from there? I had seventeen flat tires between Pennsylvania and San Francisco.

I run out of gas with fifteen cents in my pocket on Van Ness Avenue. Didn't know a soul. No job. But I made it to Market Street in February in 1934, and the steel didn't start going up until April. Well, I had a hell of a time trying to make it until the bridge started. Luckily, I happened to be down on Market Street, and I knew a couple of guys, and I run into them, and who come along with them but Jim Ward. Well, Jim Ward looked at me, and he had heard about me and he knew that I had been back east, but we had never met. He says, "Joe, you look like you could stand a meal under your belt."

I says, "Are you telling me?" and he handed me a five-dollar bill. You know, I never paid that damn money back. I forgot all about him ever giving it to me, and he never asked me for it. That's the type of man he was.

I finally had to sell my car. Paid $1,900 for it in 1929 and sold it in '34 for $87. I remember the first day I drove it out of the garage and down to Alliquippa, Pennsylvania, alongside the street cars and people looking at me, and I said to myself, well—actually, I felt out of place, honest to god.

About Jim Ward, he went into Hartford, and it seems to me—the only way I can figure—they were erecting what was supposed to be the longest single-cantilever span ever erected, and they were out beyond the falsework when they picked this girder up. Evidently the tag line might have broke or the wind got it, and the girder swung in and hit the falsework underneath, and the falsework collapsed and everything went down. There were seventeen men killed, and Jim Ward was one of them. He was close to sixty at the time. He was superintendent on the job.

Some of the men on the San Francisco Bay Bridge job, friends of mine, rented an apartment up on Ellis Street. They were born and raised back in the middlewest and from the south back on the farm, and they knew what pork meant. They knew how to get it and how to butcher it, so they take off up the damn country one night and they got themselves a pig. They took it up to the apartment and put it in the bathtub and started to butcher it. No hot water, only what you could get out of the tap. They blocked the damn bath tub up, the commode was stopped up, the sink was plugged up. Well, they got run out of the apartment, damn near got arrested. The manager run them out: "Get that damn pig out of there." They were drunk. They didn't know what the hell they were doing.

It was Friday night, payday, and you know Tower W-3, if you were walking down the catwalk from Tower 2? You can go down from Tower 3 to Tower 2 on the catwalk and then down to the Embarcadero. If you done that you'd have to wait in line to get your check, so Hank, he decides to climb down where an inch-and-a-half line was hanging down all the way to the pier—about 520 feet. He got ahold of this hemp line. I just come by when I saw him climbing over the rail, and says, "Hank, I wouldn't do that if I was you." I says, "That's a new hemp line and has quite a bit of oil in it." (It's the hemp itself.) He starts down and he came down maybe two hundred feet o.k., then all at once he started to twirl—it's only natural for a line to go the lay of the rope. Then he goes faster. Then he started to burn, see, and he had his gloves on, and then he really went. He hit the pier and that was all. The leather on his gloves was burned, and all the flesh off his hands to the bone. His legs were wrapped around the line and it burned right through to the leg bone. We used to slide down the lead cables on the jumping falls, and they were five-eighths inch apiece. At quitting time we'd climb down inside the hammerhead and then grab them two cables and slide down from 500 feet every night. These were steel cables.

Buck Weichert, Joe Walton's roommate

Do you remember the Barrel House, Pete? Well, they had a hell of a long bar in there. I think that bar must have been 150 feet long. They had a lunch counter—mostly hot dogs and chili and stuff like that—and then in the back they had a gambling joint. Well, all the fellows on the bridge liked to gamble, so they were losing their money, see. Too many sharkies in there, so they and Whitey Reeves and Ward Cartee said, "Why the hell don't we start a game ourselves, rent a room down there somewhere below the Barrel House, and we'll run a square game and give the fellows a square deal, and maybe we can make a little money, too." So we got together, built a damn table with all the fixin's and rented one of those offices up there on the third floor. Got the table all set up and we had a lawyer who knew the police and was supposed to fix up things. Everything was supposed to be copacetic. Well, we got the word that we could open up. Everything was going to be o.k. We could open up at two o'clock. Some of the guys got there early. All at once there was a knock on the door—the cops. Most of us got out the back window and down the fire escape, but a couple of guys got caught and spent the night in jail. That was the end of our gambling joint.

After all the cable was spun, they took the shims out of the outside shoes—the shoes were oval shaped fittings that held loops of cable wire—on the center anchorage. The shoes were offset like in an eccentric, and then after all the cable was spun they'd take the shims out for a final adjustment. But what happened one day in the morning, the sun came up towards Oakland and that side of the cable, the sun heated it, see, and a sudden cold spell came in from the Golden Gate, and it hit the other side of the cable. Expansion caused that shoe to flip over off that eccentric and when it did, I was just crawling underneath the main cable on the catwalk. It sounded like a missile going off. When that cable slipped off, the whole 472 wires in that strand came loose. That ruined that cable strand. They condemned it, and they had to take it all out and re-spin the whole strand. When they cut it out they threw it in the Bay. Then they had to send divers down and get it all out because the ships would come in and anchor, see, and when they would go to pull up the anchors, up would come the cable wire. The shipping companies started raising hell, and the American Bridge Company had to pull it all out. Each single wire was as thick as a lead pencil and there were 17,464 of them in each cable.

A quick crap game after work on the company tugboat.

*Bridgemen Buck
McGuinnes and Jake
Daly at catwalk com-
pletion ceremony*

We had two guy derricks up there on the center anchorage, and Pacific Bridge
Company wanted to use those derricks to pour concrete with. They hoisted it up
from the barges down below, you know. American Bridge wouldn't let them use
the derricks unless they had one of the American Bridge Company men on each
derrick. So one night they had the forms all finished. We found a pair of shoes, and
just for the hell of it we packed these shoes on the outside face of the anchorage
with the soles facing so that when they stripped the forms there would be these
shoe soles. After they poured the concrete and stripped the forms, they saw these
two shoes there and said, "My god, there's a man in there." So they got the jack
hammers and everything. They had to strip all the concrete and all they got were
two shoes. That's when the word got around to the newspapers that a man was
buried in the center anchorage.

Peter Stackpole with movie camera, atop
S.F.-Oakland Bay Bridge, 1935

Bridgeman Joe Walton and Photographer Peter Stackpole

Excerpts from a tape interview in Walton's home in San Rafael, California, in 1971. Stackpole's friend, James P. O'Neill, was also present.

Walton

I said to myself, I'll bet this kid is a reporter and he'd like to go out there and take pictures. I told him, "Just get in line and don't say nothing to nobody and we'll get on the boat and I'll show you how to get out on the pier and up on the towers." After I took him out I showed him how to come up the ladder and he got up on the top.

Stackpole

As I recall, the first time I climbed a tower I only got to the road level.

Walton

Well, then, the next time you came up you went all the way. I was in the hammerhead with the gang. Opposite me they gave you a hard time, kinda shunted you out of the way or something. Then he came over into our side, I think the next day, and I told him where to get and where to stand, and then one time—I think it was up top—we had the saddle over the hole so you couldn't climb up there—you couldn't get there except by going up the outside. This is up some 500 feet, see, and he had to climb up top.

Stackpole

Let me explain what he was just saying. I could get to the last crosspiece under the top of the tower on ladders going zigzag, but there was no way to get through the hole going to the top of the tower because the cable saddle covered the hole. So the only other way was on an iron ladder tied on by a couple of pieces of cable with cable clamps, and that damn thing, when you stepped on

Joe Walton died at the age of 80 on July 29, 1984.—Ed.

it would clank and rattle against the outside surface of the tower, and all my friends were 30 feet above me. I had no way to get to them, so I began to chicken out. I had a camera bag around me and I thought, "My god! What if I faint or pass out or something!" I'd never frozen yet and I looked up and saw Joe there so they lowered a line. I tied that line around me, and then I climbed up the last thirty feet while they took up the slack. Then I felt safe. That was the hariest thing I ever did.

Walton Then after that he was all right. He was on his own then. I figured he was a young fellow and had a job to do trying to make a living, and I thought, why not help him out. He hung around our gang because our gang was more or less friendly towards him, and I think our gang wanted to have their pictures taken as much as he wanted to take them. But he was a good fellow. We all remarked about him—how much guts he had to come out the first time—and then we become real friends after that.

Peter Stackpole, 1935

The Bridge Builders
A Portfolio of Photographs

Plate 1
The beginning of a tower, with only two sections in place

Plate 2
*Early in the construction of the cantilever
section*

Plate 3
*From below road level, inside a tower
crosspiece*

Plate 4
The beginning of a tower, before the installation of the hammerhead derrick

Plate 5
*Signalman directing placement of a load,
early in tower construction*

Plate 6
*Working on the waterfront concrete anchor-
age; hardhats are absent.*

Plate 7
From a tower top, out on a cross beam

Plate 8
*Tower construction with hammerhead
derrick in place*

Plate 9
*At the base of a tower; note the ladders
inside the cross beams.*

Plate 10
*A finished tower, ready for the catwalk and
cable spinning*

Plate 11
A tower base

Plate 12
*Looking down to the 45° angle of a tower
cross beam*

Plate 13
*On Tower W6 signalman Frank Moore
supervises the raising of a load.*

Plate 14
On a work platform at a cross beam connection, a bridgeman heats a supply of rivets.

Plate 15
A section of a tower being raised and guided into place; each of these sections weighed forty tons.

Plate 16
*Bridgeman guiding a new section into place
over their heads; they would fix it in position
from the inside.*

Plate 17
Looking up to an arm of the hammerhead derrick; the section at the bottom is suspended directly over Stackpole's head.

Plate 18
Bridgemen completing the assembly of the
hammerhead derrick

Plate 19
Bridgemen posing for Stackpole as he climbs
toward the opening at a tower top

Plate 20
Hank Dennington and others on payday at
the paymaster shack located at the base of
Tower W2

Plate 21
*Constructing the cable guide tower; this is
the last bridge contact for the cable before it
is led into the concrete anchorage.*

Plate 22
*Riding an empty block down at quitting
time; Walton is on the right.*

Plate 23
*Inside a tower truss a "heater" waits for a
call from above.*

Plate 24
*Bridgeman in skip box waits while final
rivets are placed in the tower top.*

Plate 25
Riveter without safety belt finishing off a tower plate

Plate 26
Team of riveters on the outside surface of a
tower

Plate 27
*Quitting time on the base construction site
for Tower W3*

Plate 28
Alongside the center anchorage, looking west

Plate 29
*Bridgeman boarding an elevator for a ride
up or down*

Plate 30
Signalman on center anchorage

Plate 31
*Constructing roadbed support on cantilever
section*

Plate 32
*Construction of top roadbed viewed from
the lower deck*

Plate 33
*Watching a load of rivets coming up against
the backdrop of San Francisco in 1935*

Plate 34
A properly outfitted bridgeman with hard hat, heavy gloves, spiked wrenches and safety line

Plate 35
Fitting together sections of the deck span

Plate 36
Adjusting scaffolding for riveting operation

Plate 37
Quitting time on the base of Tower W3; kegs
contain rivets

Plate 38
*On center anchorage, a stack of I-bars await
installation.*

Plate 39
*"Riding the load up"; the section will fit into
the opening where the derrick is visible.*

Plate 40
*Tower being constructed around centrally
located hammerhead derrick; the derrick
was counterbalanced by cable to enormous
concrete blocks.*

Plate 41
On the top deck of the cantilever section

Plate 42
Adjusting a cable on a derrick being used to
raise the cantilever section

Plate 43
Preparing for a ride down on an empty block

Plate 44
Leaving riveting scaffold at Yerba Buena
construction site; Joe Walton is on the right.

Plate 45
Jake Daly said, "Hey! Take my picture!"

Plate 46
View from top deck of cantilever section,
after completion of three towers

Plate 47
*Four finished towers as viewed from Yerba
Buena Island*

Plate 48
San Francisco waterfront viewed through a
cable saddle on Tower W3

Plate 49
In a skip box, workmen slacken a cable that will be used to pull the catwalk to the tower top.

Plate 50
*Looking down through the unfinished
catwalk*

Plate 51
Installing a section of the catwalk

Plate 52
*A section of catwalk before it was tightened
and had handrails added*

Plate 53
*I-bar protruding from a cable saddle; after
the attachment of a shoe it will be ready to
receive cable.*

Plate 54
Deep in contemplation, a crew goes home
after hearing the news of a fatality.

Plate 55
*Out over the side of the catwalk; Stackpole's
foot shows at lower left center.*

Plate 56
In his haste to get to the paymaster, Hank Dennington slid down one of these hemp lines.

Plate 57
Tying down the edges of the catwalk

Plate 58
Tower with cable saddles in place and
catwalk support cables

Plate 59
Tightening the stiffeners for the catwalk support cables

Plate 60
*Above the passing ferries a section of
catwalk is prepared for cable spinning.*

Plate 61
Removing empty spool during cable spinning

Plate 62
*Grabbing two strands of cable from the
passing spinning wheel*

Plate 63
Placing a loop of cable wire on the spinning wheel at the Yerba Buena anchorage; only a few strands of wire have been laid down.

Plate 64
Overview of cable spinning operation

Plate 65
Guiding the removal of an empty cable spool

Plate 66
*Beginning of cable spinning at the San
Francisco anchorage*

Plate 67
From Tower W2, a finished cable can be seen; it remains only to be wrapped and pressed into a perfect circle.

Plate 68
*View from a ferry boat passing on the north
side; to the left is the center anchorage.*

Plate 69
*Removing a catwalk support cable after
cable spinning*

Plate 70
*In between gallows frames, a bridgeman
straightens wires before banding.*

Plate 71
Heading in on the company boat

Plate 72
Gallows frames dot the catwalk as cable spinning begins between Towers W2 and W3.

Plate 73
*On Yerba Buena anchorage, men on break
from cable spinning*

Plate 74
*Roadbed truss section after attachment to
suspender cables*

Plate 75
*Ferry boat commuters, perhaps considering
the end of an era*

Plate 76
Painters giving suspender cables a first coat
of aluminum paint

Plate 77
Painting and repainting the cables is a neverending job.

Plate 78
Near the San Francisco anchorage a bridge-
man descends to street level.

Plate 79
As if by magic a section of roadway hangs between two towers.

Plate 80
*Nearing completion, with the roadway stif-
fening trusses connected into a continuous
span*

Plate 81

In 1937, the completed bridge at night. From the bridge's opening and for nearly twenty years following, a commuter train ran on the lower roadway, and automobile traffic ran in both directions on both decks. Today the train is gone, and the traffic moves only one way on each deck; the top deck going west and the lower deck going east.

Afterword:
The Man and the Bridge

Seven bridges cross San Francisco Bay, the great natural harbor that stretches north and south, paralleling the Pacific, on this country's western coast. The huge bay, with its islands, straits, subsidiary bays and inlets, is entered from the ocean by a narrow passage between rocky headlands called the Golden Gate; in its almost complete enclosure, the bay forms, virtually, an inland sea. Of the seven bridges, two are anchored in San Francisco, the city on the bay's southern headland: the San Francisco-Oakland Bay Bridge, which was completed in 1936, and the Golden Gate Bridge, completed in 1937. Both of these bridges are steel-built, wire-cable suspension bridges, marvels of twentieth-century American engineering. Both bridges were achieved as victories over the previously insurmountable difficulties the bay presented to their proponents: long spans, high winds, strong tides, deep waters, great cost. It was on the first: the longest, twin-suspension, tunneled and canti-levered, double-decked, silver-grey San Francisco-Oakland Bay Bridge that Peter Stackpole made the photographs in this portfolio.

The skyscraper and the suspension bridge—in the 20th century, lengths of steel have raised them both. Finally achieved, both became evidence, symbolic and actual, of America's will to build upward from the Depression of the 1930s. That time was the greatest time yet known for the building of both skyscraper and bridge: the tallest building the world had known, the Empire State Building, was rising in 1930; in 1933, work began on the bridge that would be the longest in the world when it was built, the San Francisco-Oakland Bay Bridge.

Two great photographic documents re-create their building for us. In Manhattan, Lewis Hine followed the "skyboys" up, up, and up as they riveted together the steel beams that would scrape the sky. At the other edge of the United States, Peter Stackpole climbed the steel suspension towers set on piers across San Francisco Bay (towers taller, from top to bottom, than the city's tallest building) and swung on catwalks with the bridgemen 450 feet above deep water. For Hine, the work on the skyscraper was his last great human document; for Stackpole, the bridge and its builders became the first subject to elicit a long essay from his camera. Both photographers put themselves in places customarily known only to workers; both produced photographs that we respond to with extraordinary emotion because of their thrilling sense of shared danger and achievement—worker and photographer, subject and artist, alike and equal in the condition of their work. It's the height that dizzies us, brings forth a visceral awe at photographs such as these. Accustomed to the street, we fear for photographer and subject alike, and our feeling elevates their work. Like the man on the tightrope, whose performance we call "walking," these men engage in work we do not consider pedestrian.

Lewis Hine's photographs of men at work on the Empire State Building are well-known. Peter Stackpole's equivalent essay on the men who built the San Francisco-Oakland Bay Bridge now has its first full publication. For many, the photographs on the preceding pages will have been seen as a revelation, although they are almost fifty years old. To be sure, they have been exhibited and published, both shortly after they were taken and in the last several years. Their first exhibition was in 1935 at the San Francisco Museum of Art. The early publication was in the July 1935 issue of *Vanity Fair:* two pages of small reproductions that gave little indication of the extent and thoroughness of Stackpole's work. Despite recent exhibitions and publications in San Francisco, Stackpole's photographs are still, in some quarters, thought to be documents of the Golden Gate Bridge, which was being raised at the same time. This book, then, also brings to public attention the *other* bridge, the San Francisco-Oakland Bay Bridge.

Peter Stackpole started his work on the Bay Bridge in 1934, when he was twenty-one, two years out of high school. Joe Walton, signalman of the raising gang that Stackpole worked with, "figured he was a young fellow and had a job to do trying to make a living." But there was no commission for Stackpole's work, and so no real promise of a "living." Gabriel Moulin, an established San Francisco photographer who operated his studio with the help of his sons, Irving and Raymond, had already been appointed the official photographer of the bridge. No, Stackpole simply came to the work because the sight of the one tower already erected and of the men beginning to raise the other three towers thrilled him, "hit him like a revelation," as he says. The beauty and danger excited him to his work, and he continued in it for two years until 1936, when he was invited by *Time* magazine to go to New York to work on a mysterious magazine "X" that was first published in November 1936 under the name *Life.*

Although he was a "young fellow," Stackpole came to the bridge well-prepared for the sort of work it would demand. He had been making photographs with a 35mm camera since 1929, and after a year of training for competitive swimming, he was in the sort of physical condition essential for the climbing and coordination that work on the bridge demanded. It was his ability with his hand-held camera, however, that in part made the sort of photographs we see here possible. He describes his beginnings as one of the pioneer American photojournalists:

"My interest in photography began in 1929 or so when I switched hobbies with a junior high-school chum who learned model airplane building from me in exchange for teaching me photography. (My friend went on into an aviation career later.) I started with an *Agfa Memo* half-frame camera, then bought my first Leica, a Model A (serial number 828) in 1929. I used both cameras to catch 'candids' of students and teachers while attending Oakland Technical High School. I became obsessed with technical experimentation in the processing and enlarging of miniature negatives during my high-school years. Nitrate films that could be wound in cassettes could be bought cheaply as short ends from motion-picture processing labs in Oakland. During those depression years, outdated paper was all I could afford. Fresh enlarging paper cost $5.50 a gross. That's why I kept the prints small—5 x 7 inches."

His "candids" were shown in an exhibition in the high school, among them one he remembers particularly: a photograph of his English teacher reading, book open in one hand. Stackpole took it through the hole for the inkwell in his classroom desk. The sense of play in the oddness of the angle, the pleasure in trying something different and making it work evident in this early photograph, have characterized his photography ever since. And the pleasure and surprise of his teacher and classmates were important, too; Stackpole has remained a photographer who needs an appreciative audience.

Stackpole's experimental use of his Leica was evident in another early photograph, made when he was working, without pay, for the Oakland *Post-Enquirer*. The photograph turned out to be a "first," not only for him, but for photojournalism as well. The occasion was a heavyweight boxing match in Oakland in the early 1930s. Max Baer, then a comer, later the world champion, fought and defeated an opponent long forgotten. The *Post-Enquirer* sent its photographers to the match. The regulars took their Speed Graphics or Graflexes; Stackpole took his Leica. They set their tripods up at a distance above the ring; Stackpole got as close to it as he could. Although his f/3.5 lens was slow, even under the bright lights he got what he was after, what his camera captured best—the action of the fight. He had to use "dynamite" developer to get his print, and it was published, although the *Enquirer's* photoengravers balked at working with so grainy an image.

His two years of apprenticeship at the *Post-Enquirer* were important preparation for his future career. The emphasis there was on the use of big cameras and the mummifying effects of the big flash lighting typical of most American newspapers of the period. But the *Enquirer*, the smallest of the Hearst chain, had bought an Ermanox, a miniature, glass-plate camera that was being used by European photographers, among them Dr. Erich Salomon for Berlin's *Illustrirte Zeitung*. In fact, it was Salomon, whose extraordinarily informal portraits of European statesmen invited the first use of the term "candid," who suggested the use of the Ermanox to William Randolph Hearst. The publisher, fearing the threat to photographers' fingers and eyes of the flash powder required by the big cameras, was glad to try the small camera, which was fast enough to be operated with available light. But few of the *Enquirer's* staff were willing to give up their customary Speed Graphics and Graflexes for the Ermanox. Stackpole used it, however, and he also learned to work with the big cameras. Still, he preferred his Leica, which was loaded with a continuous roll of film, an aid to easy manipulation. He remembers the variety of his experiences at the newspaper and their meaning for his future:

> "Before finishing high school in 1932, I found the job opportunities few. I did work part-time for the Oakland *Post-Enquirer*, a paper that doesn't exist now. I worked as an apprentice after school and on weekends. There was no salary, but the experience was invaluable. There was a man named Howard Robbins there who taught me a lot. I learned the use of larger cameras while covering sports, news events and a few murders. It was a time when newspaper photographs were usually of posed subjects, or even stock shots from the Underwood & Underwood agency. So my devotion to the possibilities that photographs of people might have a different, more spontaneous look were not views held by the newspaper's editors. They didn't go along with my conviction that there was a lot in photography that couldn't be done on a tripod. Then, too, it wasn't convenient to have a kid in the darkroom—I wasn't twenty-one yet—when reporters would bring in tins of gin after police raids, the darkroom being the ideal place to have a snort. I was fired on both counts. Fired—when there was no pay!"

While his early experience of photojournalism prepared Stackpole for work with a 35mm camera, it accounts only partially for his success on the bridge. The development of an appreciation of structural form and an eye for right composition that is evident in his bridge photographs is more difficult to trace. He had a talent, but how was it nurtured? The development of his ability to see photographs was certainly related to his association since childhood with art and artists. His father, the sculptor and muralist Ralph Stackpole, was one of the leaders of the community of artists who had their studios in what is now San Francisco's financial district. Ralph Stackpole's was at 27 Hotaling Place, a small street perpendicular to the Montgomery Block Building, the locally famous "Monkey Block," where, among others, the photographer Dorothea Lange had her studio. In 1923, Stackpole Senior had returned to San Francisco from Paris where he, his wife Adele, an artist well-known in the Bay Area, and their son had spent several years. The couple had separated in Paris; Peter and his mother lived in Oakland on their eventual return.

Traveling by ferryboat across the bay to visit his father, Peter often brought his camera and took pictures of the stoneyard below the studio. His father, who wanted him to become a sculptor, would protest, "You don't need that," and hand him a pencil and a piece of paper. In 1930, when Ralph Stackpole was making his enormous, direct-cut stone sculptures for the entrance to the San Francisco Stock Exchange, Diego Rivera came to the city to work on murals for the Exchange. The hospitable and politically liberal sculptor invited the Mexican painter, known for his Communist Party activities, to live in his studio as they both prepared to ornament this local capitalist stronghold. Peter Stackpole even posed for Rivera: he is the central figure in the mural, the youth holding an airplane. As he stood for as long as he could bear it, model airplane held high, the budding photographer may have been amused by the somewhat Mexicanized apotheosis of his pre-camera days that Rivera was creating. Among other artists who frequented Ralph Stackpole's studio was Otis Oldfield, a painter who drew scenes of shipping and the small traffic on San Francisco Bay from his cottage on Telegraph Hill. His wedding in the stoneyard was one of the important celebrations of San Francisco's colony of artists in the late 1920s.

Edward Weston was another of Ralph Stackpole's friends. They had met during the photographer's several brief residences in San Francisco during the 1920s, and the sculptor had spent some time with Weston in Mexico. Late in 1931 or early in 1932, when Weston was living in a rented studio in the center of Carmel, Ralph and Peter Stackpole drove down from San Francisco for a visit. Weston had been working on still-lifes, "a misnomer," he wrote in his *Daybook*, "for my most living artichokes, peppers, onions, cabbage." Those were among the prints that Peter Stackpole saw as Weston placed them, one by one, on the easel in his studio, moving them slowly, allowing time for his visitors to comprehend each print. He also showed them photographs of the trees and rocks of Point Lobos and some commissioned portraits. One portrait was particularly memorable to the model-airplane enthusiast: the cameraman Ivanow, known for his work on Paul Strand's and Ralph Steiner's movie, *The Plough that Broke the Plains*, at the wheel of his classy Bugatti. The afternoon spent seeing Weston's work was profoundly disturbing to the young photojournalist. The carefully studied subject, the fine grain and range of tone produced from the large negative, the congruence of intention and achievement—all these qualities of Weston's photography were very different from the "candid" shots he had been producing with his Leica.

His confusion about the validity of small-camera work was furthered by his seeing the first exhibition of an association of photographers called Group f/64 at San Francisco's De Young Museum in November, 1932. According to Weston, the group was formed "with the primary purpose of stimulating interest in real photography and encouraging new talent." By "real," Weston meant the sort of photography he had been doing since around 1922: straight, not fussed up with extra-photographic tricks, no gauze over the lens to soften the image, and everything in the photograph as clear in detail as the right lens on an 8 x 10 view camera with superior negative production and contact printing could make it. His magnificently isolated subjects implied something other than their everyday reality. The miniature, hand-held camera was not even considered in Group f/64's definition of real photography, for although amateurs had been making straight records of the world around them with one sort of miniature camera or another since the late 19th century, the prints from their negatives were customarily of drugstore quality. The fineness of the print, one of the medium's claims to artistry, accounted for at least half of the group's credo. In the face of the photographs he saw at the De Young Museum by Ansel Adams, Imogen Cunningham, Willard Van Dyke, John Paul Edwards, Edward Weston, Brett Weston, and others, it was difficult for Peter Stackpole to maintain his devotion to quite another way of seeing. Still, the example of the American photojournalist Tom McAvoy, who produced "pictures for the people" with a 35mm camera, continued to be a strong influence. At the same time,

Stackpole's knowledge of f/64 photography seems to have made him aware of the difference between making and taking a photograph, between the intended and the random.

> "Catching the world of people and events with a hand-held camera was still fascinating to me. But I felt I needed an important subject—a great big subject that a small camera could handle best. I had to wait a couple of years until I found it. When I saw the towers of the Bay Bridge going up, the clouds of uncertainty finally cleared."

His instinct proved to be right. In 1934, after he had made a number of photographs on the bridge, he showed them to Willard Van Dyke, the most forceful organizer of Group f/64. It was in his Brockhurst Gallery in Oakland that members exhibited their photographs. Van Dyke had studied briefly with Edward Weston in Carmel in 1929; he was devoted to the sense of Weston's photography. Weston, untypically, was consistent in his admiration of the younger man. He "knew enough," Weston commented, "to make me feel that I had little to give him." Weston thought of Van Dyke as one of those "intelligent—clean—positive" young men "who will rediscover America." Van Dyke's encouragement meant everything to Stackpole; with it, the bridge images "poured out of the darkroom," as he puts it.

Willard Van Dyke's interest in Peter Stackpole's enthusiasm for photography had begun several years earlier. They had met at the gallery, which Van Dyke and Mary Jeannette Edwards directed. So great was the Brockhurst directors' devotion to straight photography, to the sort Weston was producing and that eventually would be formulated and promulgated by the manifestos of Group f/64, that in 1931 they held an exhibition at Brockhurst with the anacronistic title, *First Salon of Pure Photography.* When Van Dyke and Stackpole met, they discovered that they shared not only their concerned interest in the possibilities of photography, but also that strangely strong bond that frequently occurs in American life, their devotion to the inspired teaching of the same, favorite high-school teacher. At first, recognizing the aspiring photographer's talent and determination, but also sensing his need of direction, the older man was mentor to the younger; in time, he became a friend, and remains one today.

In 1934, when Peter Stackpole was able to show his friend examples of his work on the bridge, Willard Van Dyke was struck by their uniqueness, their freshness, and by the extraordinary quality of the eye behind them. He admired the thoroughness of the documentation, the hard-won, step-by-step portrayal of the men and the bridge as the work progressed. To him, the photographs seemed "less studied," more alive and original, than any documentary series he had seen. His admiration extended to the quality of the 5 x 7 prints that Stackpole had taken pains to produce. In Van Dyke's estimation, "No one made better prints from a 35mm negative than Peter Stackpole." Stackpole was determined to prove that enlargements from a 35mm negative could be as sharp as 8 x 10 contact prints.

On the strength of the bridge photographs, Van Dyke proposed that Peter Stackpole join Group f/64. He believed that the group should expand and attract younger members.

While Ansel Adams objected on the ground that only photographers committed to the entire f/64 formulation should be admitted, Stackpole was accepted as a member. Actually, his membership was nominal. The only three exhibitions of the group ever held (at the De Young Museum, at Adam's Danysh Gallery in San Francisco, and at the Denny/Wattrous Gallery in Carmel) were already in the past. And Weston, for one, was beginning to disassociate himself from what was, after all, not so much an organization as a company of like-minded friends. But the designation as a member had real significance for Stackpole then: it meant that Van Dyke's admiration was confirmed by his invitation to join, if in name only, the photographers who produced what he believed to be the best contemporary photography on the West Coast. Peter Stackpole had found what every young artist needs: an admiring audience, and one that he could reciprocally admire.

The bridgemen moved on and up as their work progressed. Accompanying them, Stackpole shook any confusion that f/64 style had induced about how to treat his subject. As the bridgemen rode steel beams high above the bay, he photographed them from his vantage point on an equally high crosswalk: he kept up with them. Balancing himself, camera in hand, was difficult; a tripod would have been dangerous baggage. At first, the men wanted portraits of themselves: "Hey! Take my picture!" He sold them prints for 25¢ each. As he grew accustomed to the footwork, his photographs became freer. He was able to see the detail as well as the drama, to produce photographs that tell us about high-steel construction methods of the 1930s as few others do. We see the men bolting, then riveting the lengths of steel together, a method that has been superceded by welding. Men catch hot rivets in a cup as they are thrown by the tender of the heating oven to be hammered into place. The air is steamy; the noise of the big hammer constant. Bridgemen lean across a void to shove beams into place, ride the steel as it is moved by cranes, jump onto elevators over a long drop to the water. Now there are government safety boards to overrule activities such as these. Some men in the photographs wear hard hats; some longshoremen's caps. The hard hats are the men of the American Bridge Company; the soft hats are occasional workers. The latter were expendable, there being so many who needed the job in those Depression years. The hard hats carried safety ropes on their belts; ropes weren't issued to other workers. The photographs also tell us that no black men worked on the bridge.

There were five consecutive steps in the building of the twin-suspension part of the bridge, the section that spans the water between San Francisco and Yerba Buena Island: laying the foundation piers, building the towers, stringing the catwalks across them, spinning the wire cable, hanging the decks. Peter Stackpole started his document with the second step, the first being accessible only to the photographer underwater, a realm he did not conquer until about twelve years later. The portrayal of the remaining steps form chapters in his documentary volume. After the steel towers were raised, the great cable saddles were placed at their tops. We now admire the saddles for their powerful form; they were state-of-the-art casting then, the largest single castings used in bridge building to that time. We see the bridgemen, spiders making their webs, inch forward with the wire-mesh catwalks, stiffening them with boards as they go. Then comes the spinning of the cable, the primitive-looking wheel moving back and forth between the towers until 7,464 wires are in place. We see the powerful machine that compresses the wires with the force of six 75-ton jacks to make them into the cables on which the flexibility and strength of the bridge will depend.

The episode of cable spinning, from July 1935 to mid-January 1936, forms the third chapter of Stackpole's document. He also recorded the cable spinning on movie film. As a beginning, he borrowed a movie camera and, with careful economy, shot four rolls of film during the steel-raising phase of construction. Columbia Steel Company on seeing his film commissioned one on cable spinning and provided him with a Cine-Kodak Special.

The year 1935 was an especially productive one. Stackpole prepared some twenty-five prints for his exhibition at the San Francisco Museum of Art, which attracted favorable attention to his ongoing project. At the suggestion of Imogen Cunningham, he sent some of the bridge photographs to Frank Crowninshield, editor of *Vanity Fair*, who published them in the July 1935 issue. The *Oakland Tribune* noticed his work and gave him an assignment that changed the course of his career: he was sent to cover, in his candid way, the Charter Day ceremonies at the University of California, Berkeley. President Roosevelt's Secretary of Labor, Frances Perkins, addressed the audience; ex-President Herbert Hoover received an honorary degree. As Madame Secretary spoke, Hoover dozed, and Stackpole caught him napping. The view was too candid for the *Tribune* to publish, but a sympathetic city editor suggested that Stackpole send a print to *Time* magazine, which was pleased to publish it. Assignments then started to come from Time Inc. publications. Among them was one from the editors of *Fortune.* They wanted an informal essay on William Randolph Hearst, to be made at Wyntoon, the publisher's 50,000 acre settlement in California near the Oregon border. A number of the photographs, which were published in *Fortune's* October 1935 issue, were made in Dufay color, a forerunner of Kodachrome. They were the first examples of 35mm color to be published by the magazine. All in all, the assignment was a strenuous test for the twenty-two-year-old photographer; although it "scared" him, he apparently got over his fright. His views of life at Wyntoon, from which Hearst ran his twenty-eight newspapers, include the Disneylike variety of architecture, from Bavarian to Tudor to California ranch. Stackpole caught the tycoon at his amusements—playing croquet, playing tennis, patting his dachshund. He brought back intimate views of Hearst's visitors—his eminent ones and his pretty ones—of his retinue and retainers, even one of his collection of Bavarian hats. Many of the captions published with the photographs were developed from Stackpole's observations of his subjects. Hearst was pleased, and as for Time Inc., Stackpole had passed the test. He became a stringer for *Time* magazine, sending them photographs of notable visitors to the San Francisco area.

Stackpole continued his work on the bridge as the demands on his time—demands that had evolved out of his committment to the bridge—and the summer winds and fog of San Francisco would permit. One of the oddest projects of the period was his construction of a thirty-foot, balsa-wood scale model of the bridge, which he built in sections in his mother's house in Oakland. The model was commissioned by Timothy Phluger, the architect of the San Francisco approach to the bridge. Eventually it was displayed in San Francisco's Ferry Building, where commuters, fresh off the boats that had brought them so pleasantly to San Francisco from ports around the East Bay, could see the shape of their future.

It wasn't long before work on the bridge was over. The last rivet was hammered into place on October 23, 1936; on November 12, President Roosevelt sent a telegraphic signal from Washington that opened the bridge to traffic. The bridgemen moved on to other high-steel construction, and Stackpole found photographic work that paid, first in Los Angeles and then in New York. While the men had built a bridge across San Francisco Bay, he had made, by his document of their work, a bridge to his future.

His "big subject," the Bay Bridge, so right for his development as a photographer in 1934, in time was recognized as the outstanding achievement of bridge construction in twentieth-century America. In 1955, the American Society of Civil Engineers named it one of the Seven Wonders of Engineering. Among other attributes, the Society cited the advancement of engineering design it represented, particularly the design and construction of the concrete island that forms its central anchorage, Chief Engineer Charles H. Purcell's great triumph. The bridge's unprecedented length, six miles from western to eastern approach, four of them over water, and its service to the communities around the bay were also considered. A judgment that recalled the Wonders of the Ancient World also figured in the engineers' citation: the structure's "capacity to excite public wonder."

Public awe has always been excited by bridges; myth and legend have surrounded and enhanced our perception of them. Their image occurs to us in times of apprehensive anticipation and of possible regret: "Don't cross your bridges before you come to them," we say. And, "Don't burn your bridges behind you." In Germanic legend, the first bridge was a rainbow between Valhalla and Earth. Folklore of all nations and tribes contains bridges of strange appearance and miraculous properties: made of ivory, glass, or gold; supporting the good, giving way under evil. Almost impassibly narrow and even invisible bridges tested Arthurian heroes; there are fabulous bridges that contain human bodies in their foundations as assurance of their holding fast against the demons of the water. In Western poetry and prose, from the Renaissance to the present, the bridge is used as a metaphor for the most important passages, from life to death, Earth to paradise or purgatory, idea to action, dream to reality. One of the world's most honored titles, derived from the ancient Roman priesthood, is Pontifex Maximus. It means "greatest bridge builder."

Bridges have also figured importantly in the works of painters and topographical artists in the modern Western world. In the twentieth century, artists have been drawn to them and to other industrial structures because of their engineered beauty as well as their symbolic power. As the century advanced, a democratic interest in the men who actually put the structures together became predominant. The American artist Joseph Pennell gave a passionate account of his desire to illustrate the construction of another of the Seven Modern Wonders, the Panama Canal:

> "I went to the Panama Canal because I believed the greatest engineering work
> the world has ever seen would give me the greatest artistic inspiration of my life.
> I went because I believed that the Canal I should see the Wonder of Work, the

Picturesqueness of Labor, realized on the grandest scale. I believed that if but little of all I had heard of the huge locks, the great dam, the deep cut, were true, I should find the most marvelous subjects of all time, so risked it."

Pennell's impulse to go to Panama in 1912 foreshadows the attraction of American artists to similar subjects in the 1930s. Some were encouraged by their work for the government's Works Progress Administration; others, like Stackpole, came to the subject on their own. During this period, artists produced works titled *Steelworker, Heavy Industry, Derricks, Bridge Repairs, Pneumatic Drill*, and murals that might include any or all of these. The power and energy of structures created by twentieth-century engineers was seen as beautiful, a beauty accentuated by contemporary political and social circumstances. The men who built them were seen as crucial to the subject. A Pontifex Maximus was no longer singled out in the portrayal; it was extended to a group of tough, hard-working bridgemen in hard hats. Peter Stackpole's photographs of them as they were building the San Francisco-Oakland Bay Bridge epitomize intentions, social and artistic, of that time and place, mid-1930s America. Now, after seeing it whole almost fifty years later, we can realize that his document of the bridge and its builders is one of the most valuable works we have in twentieth-century American photography.

—Anita Ventura Mozley
Menlo Park, July 1984

Sources

Quotations and Comments

Gould, Robert Sewall, Civil Engineer. Comments on working conditions by a man who was hired as a cable spinner, July 1984.

Pennell, Joseph. Quotation from Kiehl, David W. *Working America: Industrial Imagery in American Prints, 1900-1940.* New York: Metropolitan Museum of Art, 1983.

Stackpole, Peter. "Background Information." Oakland, Ca.: 1983. Manuscript.

Van Dyke, Willard. Quotations and comments on Peter Stackpole's photographs from an interview, 19 July 1984.

Weston, Edward. *The Daybooks of Edward Weston*, Vol. 2. New York: Horizon, 1961.

History

Dillon, Richard. *High Steel: Building the Bridges Across San Francisco Bay.* Millbrae, Ca.: Celestial Arts, 1979.

Finch, J. Kip. "Seven Modern Wonders Named." *Civil Engineering* 25 (October, 1955): 33ff.

Fout, John, Sandra S. Phillips, Susan Fillin Yeh. *Picture Magazines Before Life.* Woodstock, N.Y.: Catskill Center for Photography, 1982.

Gilliam, Harold. *San Francisco Bay.* Garden City, N.Y.: Doubleday, 1957.

Hicks, William. *Words and Pictures: An Introduction to Photojournalism.* New York: Harper and Row, 1952.

Kouwenhoven, John A. *Made in America.* Garden City, N.Y.: Doubleday, 1948.

Purcell, Charles H. "The Construction Story." *Purcell Pontifex, A Tribute.* Privately printed in a limited edition, San Francisco, 1937.

————. "Great San Francisco-Oakland Bay Bridge Will Be Completed, August 1936." *San Francisco-Oakland Bay Bridge.* San Francisco: Columbia Steel Company, 1935.

Steinman, David B., and Sara Ruth Watson. *Bridges and Their Builders.* New York: Putnam, 1941.

Trachtenberg, Alan. *Brooklyn Bridge, Fact and Symbol.* 2d ed. Chicago and London: University of Chicago Press, 1979.

Watson, Wilbur J. and Sara Ruth Watson. *Bridges in History and Legend.* Cleveland: Jansen, 1937.

Glossary

Anchorage: In the cable-spinning operation, the cable would be led into huge concrete emplacements, wrapped around shoes on I-bars embedded in the concrete and then led out again. Later the opening would be filled in with more concrete, anchoring the cable. On the west side, the suspension side, there are three anchorages: San Francisco, the center anchorage and Yerba Buena.

Bight: The tension in a pulley system

Cantilever section: The east side of the bridge, between Yerba Buena Island and Oakland, is a cantilever structure. Rather than being suspended as the west side is, this section is composed of members projected out over the water from end supports, with secondary support from a series of over thirty piers.

Catwalk: Wire scaffolding strung between towers and used in the assembling of the cable-spinning apparatus.

Derrick: A large crane for hoisting and moving heavy objects

Eccentric: A metal casting that is out of round, or has one end larger than the other, or has its anchor off-center

Falls *(set of):* The mechanisms of a pulley block

Falsework: A temporary support structure

Gallows Frames: Cable-spinning supports and guides hung on the catwalk

Load Block: Guide castings in a pulley system

Member: Any beam, bar or component piece of a larger structure

Niggerhead: Component of the pulley system on a traveler

Reave: To thread cable or line

Saddle: A cable guide and cable weight support

Shims: Thin, tapered pieces of wood or metal used to fill spaces between construction components

Shoes: A casting used as an anchorage for cable

Slag: The residue from ore-processing

Strain: Creating tension in a cable

Stripping forms: Removal of the wood molds after concrete has set

Tag line: A line attached to a load being raised; used to control lateral movement

Traveler: A hoist on rails

Truss: A support framework

Note on tower numbers: Reference is made to six towers (W1 through W6) on the west side or suspension side of the bridge. Only four are actual towers: W2, W3, W5 and W6. W1 is a support pier and does not go above deck height. W4 is the center anchorage.

Notes on the Photographs

The photographs were taken with Model C and Model F Leica cameras.

The lenses used were the 50mm Elmar and the 35mm Elmar, both non-coated lenses.

Films used were DuPont and Eastman nitrate, loaded from bulk film.

The developer was modified Sease III formula, which gave a one-stop loss of film speed, but was considered the best at that time for fine-grain results. The formula was mixed in Stackpole's darkroom.

A Weston II meter was used.

A University finder made careful framing possible.

Early prints were made on Defender Velour Black Paper, double-weight glossy.

Page 22
Buck Weichert was to later lose his life in a fall from the upper deck to the lower deck on the cantilever span.

Page 24
McGuinnes is holding a piece of cable wire in his hand. All the bridgemen were "awarded" a clipping at the ceremony.

Page 26
Stackpole used the movie camera to make a film on cable spinning for the Columbia Steel Company.

Plate 1
This photograph was taken on Stackpole's first day out.

Plate 7
Note the loose rivets on scaffolding. Workers were killed and injured by rivets and other material that rolled or were knocked off from higher level work areas.

Plate 8

The bars sticking through the metal plate were used to fix the plate in position on the framework. Later these bars were replaced with rivets.

Plate 12

This was taken near quitting time. The two boats are company tugs coming to pick up the men working out on the tower.

Plate 14

On a signal from above these hot rivets would be sent up to the riveting site through the pneumatic hoses seen at the left.

Plate 18

At a certain juncture in the construction of a tower, a derrick would be assembled on the top of the completed section. It would then be used to construct the next section of the tower. At the finish of each stage the derrick would be moved higher up.

Plate 20

Hank Dennington is the worker who lost his life sliding down the 500 ft. hemp rope that was too oily for a good grip.

Plate 21

The guide towers move to accommodate expansion and contraction of the cable.

Plate 24

To the left is the cable saddle. It would be moved into the position where the men are shown working, and the construction of the catwalk and the cable spinning operation could begin.

Plate 26

A riveting operation consisted of an outside team and a team inside the tower wall. On the inside a "sticker" would place the red hot rivet into a hole, and a "bucker upper" would hold it in place for the outside riveters.

Plate 29

These elevators moved on cables the entire distance from the base of the tower to the top—518 ft. They would sway in the wind, and often it was very difficult to get on, as well as off.

Plate 43

The practice of holding the block while others got on was known as "overhauling the load." Often it was very difficult to get an empty block to move.

Plate 44

In this and other photographs note the absence of Treasure Island. Construction of this man-made island had not yet begun.

Plate 45

Jake Daly later was seriously injured in a fall from Tower W2

Plate 47

The cable saddles can be seen at the top of the towers. They are not yet in position for the cable spinning operation to begin.

Plate 51

The catwalk was ordinary cyclone fencing. It would be brought up to the tower top in preassembled sections, and the men would push it out along the cables using their feet.

Plate 52

Because of the steep angle and the sag, climbing and walking on untightened catwalk was physically exhausting.

Plate 54

It was traditional to quit for the day when a death occurred. In this photograph, Buck Weichert, Joe Walton's roommate, sits in the center.

Plate 59

These cables later were cut up and used as suspension cables.

Plate 62

The cowbell at the hub of the spinning wheel ould clank day and night, reminding workers to duck at the approach of the wheel.

Plate 67

Each cable is composed of 17,464 parallel wires, each the diameter of a lead pencil.

Plate 70

Thirty-seven wires would be banded into a larger strand, with each strand being 5" in diameter; the finished cable would be almost 29 ft. in diameter.

Plate 75

The nearly completed span can be seen reflecting in the cabin windows

Plate 76

Cable painters were called "spidermen."

Plate 78

At night navigating these beams was a dangerous business. At least one worker mistakenly stepped out into space and fell to his death through the roof of a warehouse below.